Cultus, Culture, and the Nature of Identity

Rt. Rev. James D. Heiser, M.Div., S.T.M.
Bishop, the Evangelical Lutheran Diocese of North America

REPRISTINATION PRESS
MALONE, TEXAS

REPRISTINATION PRESS
716 HCR 3424 E
MALONE, TEXAS 76660

www.repristinationpress.com

ISBN 1–891469–58-4

Foreword

The following essay was presented in 2016 to the Evangelical Lutheran Diocese of North America during the annual Colloquium and Synod. It was written and presented as a continuation of a line of thought which the author began to explore with the essays published as *The One True God, The Two Kingdoms, and the Three Estates* (2011) and *Sovereignty and Authority in the Context of the American Republic* (2016). In the past year, the pressing need to address such topics has only become more apparent. The West, in general, has suffered a fundamental disorientation regarding its understanding of the relationship between *cultus* and culture. The author has few illusions regarding his ability to address this larger disorientation, but these essays have been written in the hope of offering some guidance to his readers in an examination of the issues which are currently at stake.

+James D. Heiser
Bishop, The Evangelical Lutheran Diocese of North America
Malone, Texas

If one is looking for the origins of culture and its connection to identity, one is driven to examine the very roots of the divisions of mankind and the consciousness of historic time. The distinction between historic time and mythic time is vital to understanding the significance of myth in the formation of identity. In the words of Mircea Eliade:

> Myth narrates a sacred history; it relates an event that took place in primordial Time, the fabled time of the 'beginnings.' In other words, myth tells how, through the deeds of Supernatural Beings, a reality came into existence, be it the whole of reality, the Cosmos, or only a fragment of reality—an island, a species of plant, a particular kind of human behavior, an institution. Myth, then, is always an account of a "creation"; it relates how something was produced, began to *be*. ... The actors in myth are Supernatural Beings.[1]

Historic time is thus the time in which human beings are perceived to be actors; although 'Supernatural Beings' may still influence their actions, records of historic time are perceived in a substantially different way from the perception of mythic time. The events of myth are not perceived simply as past events; rather, they have an enduring significance for those who believe the myth. The individual living in the present may perceive himself to be participating in the mythic event by means of ritual. The study of historic time may be a font of

1   Mircea Eliade, *Myth and Reality*, trans. by Willard R. Trask, (Long Grove, Illinois: Waveland Press, Inc., 1998) p. 5–6.

8

information such that one may learn from the 'lessons of the past,' nevertheless the events of the historic time remain fundamentally unrepeatable past events.[2]

The history of the Greeks and Romans[3] points to two events as the beginning of the present age of man—events which Herodotus identifies as distinguishing between *spatium historicum* and *spatium mythicum*: the Trojan War and the first Olympiad.[4] Herodotus works from a "Homeric conception of the deep past as a time inaccessible to normal human knowledge ... the Muses do have knowledge (ἴστε) about this heroic past, whereas we hear only report (κλέος οἶον ἀκούομεν) and do not know anything (οὐδέ τι ἴδμεν)."[5] The Muses, proclaiming that which purportedly had been revealed to them by the gods, reveal that which is bound up with the *cultus* of Greek pagan antiquity. That which is myth is not fictional; rather, it was understood to be that record of events which is revealed by the gods. The transition between *spatium mythicum* and *spatium historicum* is thus immediately connected with the transition which is now know as the Catastrophe which is the meeting point of the Bronze and Iron Ages around 1,200 B.C., a time

---

2   For more on the distinction between myth, sacred history and secular history, please see the author's book, *A Time for Every Purpose Under Heaven—An Exploration of Sacred History* (Malone, Texas: Repristination Press, 2012).

3   "For Rome to become a world empire it was essential that the Romans become part of the time schemes of the Greeks, and the work that went on to make this happen was collaborative work." Denis Feeney, *Caesar's Calendar—Ancient Time and the Beginnings of History*, (Berkeley: University of California Press, 2007) p. 5.

4   ibid., p. 72, 81.

5   ibid., p. 74.

when the eastern Mediterranean was ravaged by "a general pattern of destruction by fire, and both the logic and data indicate that the sites were raged by well-armed enemies."[6] The end of the Bronze Age is a time in which the civilizations which existed to that point in time are largely swept away, and with their end comes a termination of the period known at the time of heroes.

Hesiod (ca. 750–ca. 650 B.C.) divided the history of man into five ages or 'races.' Of those five races or ages or man, three—the Golden, Silver and Bronze—had passed from the scene before his own age. The fourth 'race'—"a divine race of heroes called demigods"—had either recently passed from the scene, or were (at best) hidden from the fifth race:

> But when this race [i.e., the bronze race] was covered over by the earth, Zeus, son of Cronus, made another again, the fourth on wide-nourishing earth, better and more just. A divine race of heroes called demigods, the race before ours on the broad earth. These were destroyed by evil war and terrible battle, some under the seven gates of Thebes, the land of Cadmus, as they fought over the cattle of Oedipus; others were destroyed after traveling in ships across the broad deep of the sea, because of lovely-haired Helen. Some of them were embraced by death, but others were granted customs and a life apart from men by father Zeus, son of Cronus, dwelling at the ends of the earth. These live with carefree minds in the islands of the

6   Robert Drews, *The End of the Bronze Age—Changes in Warfare and the Catastrophe CA. 1200 B.C.,* (Princeton: Princeton University Press, 1993) p. 84.

blessed beyond the deep-eddying Ocean. They are the
blessed heroes, for whom the fertile land willing bears
sweet-smelling fruit three times a year.[7]

As noted, this fourth race had, in Hesiod's estimation, in part
passed from the world, and in part had retreated beyond the
reaches of the fifth race to the "islands of the blessed." As for
the race which constitutes the men now known upon the earth,
Hesiod declares: "I wish I did not live among the fifth people!
If only I had already died or was born later. For the race now
is iron. Never will they cease from miserable toil by day nor
from being distressed by night. The gods will give them difficult worries, but they will mix goods with the evils. Zeus will
destroy even this race of chattering people when they are born
with grey hair."[8]

It is thus that the fourth race passes from historic time,
and its remnants inhabit only mythic spaces outside of time.
And it falls to Aeneas, the last demigod and survivor of the
Trojan War, to be the one who "brings world history in his per-
son to intersect with the site of Rome… the arrival of Jupiter's
favored Trojans definitely marks the end of the local Golden
Age."[9] And this juncture of myth and history provides a classic
example of what has been described as the "most important"
attribute of ethnic identity: common ancestry from a famous
progenitor. In the words of Anthony Smith:

7   quoted in *Race and Ethnicity in the Classical World—An Anthology
of Primary Sources in Translation*, selected and trans. by Rebecca F. Ken-
nedy, C. Sydnor Roy and Max L. Goldman, (Indianapolis & Cambridge:
Hacket Publishing Company, 2013) p. 13.
8   ibid.
9   Feeney, p. 162.

Most important, it is myths of common ancestry, not any fact of ancestry (which is usually difficult to ascertain), that are crucial. It is fictive descent and putative history that matters for the sense of ethnic identification. Indeed, Horowitz has likened ethnic groups to 'super-families' of fictive descent because members view their *ethnie* as composed of interrelated families, forming one huge 'family' linked by mythical ties of filiation and ancestry.[10]

The Church is blessed to have a divinely-inspired account of the division of the nations which offers not a fictive, but a factual, descent and history, and it traces the origin of the nations to a period much earlier than the Catastrophe of the twelfth century. Following the Deluge, Genesis 10 and 11 records the division of the nations from the sons of Noah. We read in Genesis 10:32 concerning the descent from Shem, Ham, and Japheth: "These were the families of the sons of Noah, according to their generations, in their nations; and from these the nations were divided on the earth after the flood." However, the descendants of the sons of Noah were not initially divided, for we read in Genesis 11: "And the whole earth was of one language, and of one speech." (v. 1) It was thus that the whole assembly of mankind journeyed from the east, and dwelt in the land of Shinar and set themselves on the path of building "a city and a tower whose top may reach into heaven…" (v. 4) The LORD then describes them: "Behold, the people are one and they have all one language" so that the LORD's response

---

10   Anthony D. Smith, *National Identity*, (Reno: University of Nevada Press, 1991) p. 22.

12

to the rebellion of man is "'Come, let Us go down and there confuse their language, that they may not understand one another's speech.' So the Lord scattered them abroad from there over the face of all the earth, and they ceased building the city." (11:7–8) Genesis thus establishes, both in the account of the Creation and in the account of the scattering of the nations at Babel, that mankind is of one common race, born of Adam. The fall of Adam is thus the fall of the entirety of the human race (Rom. 5:12), and the hope of Adam is the hope of all those of the human race who believe the promise of the Gospel (Rom. 5:18–19). The common origin of a human race divided into nations is emphasized in the account of the beginning of the apostolic ministry on Pentecost:

> And there were dwelling in Jerusalem Jews, devout men, from every nation under heaven. And when this sound occurred, the multitude came together, and were confused, because everyone heard them speak in his own language. Then they were all amazed and marveled, saying to one another, "Look, are not all these who speak Galileans? And how is it that we hear, each in our own language in which we were born? Parthians and Medes and Elamites, those dwelling in Mesopotamia, Judea and Cappadocia, Pontus and Asia, Phrygia and Pamphylia, Egypt and the parts of Libya adjoining Cyrene, visitors from Rome, both Jews and proselytes, Cretans and Arabs—we hear them speaking in our own tongues the wonderful works of God." (Acts 2:5–11)

The designation of these Jewish men as being "from every nation under heaven/απο παντος εθνους των υπο τον ουρανον" offers an opportunity to introduce the Greek notion of the *ethnoi*—a concept with a long and nuanced usage in Greek antiquity, and one which is linked with one's language as something which both identifies and shapes one's culture.

The New Testament offers ample testimony to the Jews considering themselves to be an *ethnos*. Thus, for example, the elders of Capernaum appeal to Jesus on behalf of the centurion: "And when they came to Jesus, they begged Him earnestly, saying that the one for whom He should do this was deserving, 'for he loves our nation [εθνος ημων], and has built us a synagogue.'" (Luke 7:4–5) When the Jews plotted against the Christ, Caiaphas declared: "You know nothing at all, nor do you consider that it is expedient for us that one man should die for the people [υπερ του λαου], and not that the whole nation [και μη ολον το εθνος] should perish." (John 11:49b–50) Furthermore, St. Paul, offering his defense before Felix in Acts 24, refers to "my nation/το εθνος μου" (v. 17). Meanwhile, we are told in Revelation 14:6 that the everlasting Gospel is preached "to those who dwell on the earth—to every nation, tribe, tongue, and people/επι της γης και παν εθνος και φυλην και γλωσσαν και λαον."

Already by the time of the writing of Aristotle's Politics in the mid-fourth century B.C., the concepts of *ethnos*[11], *polis*[12], and *genos*[13] had become quite intertwined. Thus we read in Politics 1276a:

11   "race, people, nation." http://biblehub.com/greek/1484.htm
12   "city." http://biblehub.com/greek/4172.htm
13   "family, race, nation." http://biblehub.com/greek/1085.htm

14

But it may similarly be asked, Suppose a set of men inhabit the same place, in what circumstances are we to consider their city to be a single city? Its unity clearly does not depend on the walls, for it would be possible to throw a single wall round the Peloponnesus; and a case in point perhaps is Babylon, and any other city that has the circuit of a nation rather than of a city [μᾶλλον ἔθνους ἢ πόλεως]; for it is said that when Babylon was captured a considerable part of the city was not aware of it three days later. But the consideration of this difficulty will be serviceable for another occasion, as the student of politics must not ignore the question, What is the most advantageous size for a city, and should its population be of one race or of several? But are we to pronounce a city, where the same population inhabit the same place, to be the same city so long as the population are of the same race [γένος], in spite of the fact that all the time some are dying and others being born, just as it is our custom to say that a river or a spring is the same river or spring although one stream of water is always being added to it and another being withdrawn from it, or are we to say that though the people are the same people for the similar reason of continuity, yet the city is a different city?[14]

14   http://www.perseus.tufts.edu/hopper/text?doc=Perseus%3
Atext%3A1999.01.0058%3Abook%3D3%3Asection%3D1276a [Referenced May 2016] Isaac declares that Aristotle's question makes it clear that a city must "be populated by one people (*ethnos*)" and "implies that the population of a city must be of the same *genos*." (Benjamin Isaac, *The Invention of Racism in Classical Antiquity*, [Princeton and Oxford: Princeton University Press, 2004] p. 120.)

A unified *polis* is one which shares the same *genos*, and, Aristotle maintained, those who were of a different *ethnos* were of a different nature. For Aristotle, the *polis* precedes the individual and is the manifestation of a state of nature which defines all its members, as may be read in 1253a:

> Hence it is evident that the state [*polis*] is a creation of nature, and that man is by nature a political animal. And he who by nature and not by mere accident is without a state, is either above humanity, or below it; he is the
>
> 'Tribeless, lawless, hearthless one,'
>
> whom Homer denounces—the outcast who is a lover of war; he may be compared to an unprotected piece in a game of draughts. ...
>
> Thus the state is by nature clearly prior to the family and to the individual,[15] since the whole is of necessity prior to the part... The proof that the state is a creation of nature and prior to the individual is that the individual, when isolated, is not self-sufficing; and therefore he is like a part in relation to the whole.[16]

As the *polis* takes priority over the individual, the various vocations found within society are determined by nature; thus, Aristotle defines the natural state of the various souls of hu-

---

15   καὶ πρότερον δὲ τῇ φύσει πόλις ἢ οἰκία καὶ ἕκαστος ἡμῶν ἐστιν.

16   *Aristotle's Politics*, trans.by Benjamin Jowett, (Oxford: Clarendon Press, 1945) p. 28–29.

16

man beings in relationship to one another: "Again, the male is by nature superior, and the female inferior; and the one rules, and the other is ruled; this principle, of necessity extends to all mankind. ... It is clear, then, that some men are by nature free, and others slaves, and that for these latter slavery is both expedient and right."[17] So too, the war of the strong upon the weak is determined by nature: "... the art of war is a natural art of acquisition, for it includes hunting, an art which we ought to practice against wild beasts, and against men who, though intended by nature to be governed, will not submit; for war of such a kind is naturally just."[18] But while among the Greeks there is a gradation of ranks, a mark of the barbarians is their status as an undifferentiated mass: "But among barbarians no distinction is made between women and slaves, because there is no natural ruler among them: they are a community of slaves, male and female. Wherefore the poets say,—'It is meet that the Hellenes should rule over barbarians;' as if they thought that the barbarian and the slave were by nature one."[19]

Remember: those who are of the same *polis* are ideally (for Aristotle, at least) to be of the same *genos* and *ethnos*. This understanding was already at work in Plato, who made the same point in his Republic when in Book Five he weighed the topic of the justice of Greek *poleis* going to war with one another. Thus 'Socrates' asserts: "Do you think it is right for Greek states [πόλεις] to sell Greeks into slavery, or to allow others to do so, so far as they can prevent it? Ought they not rather to make it their custom to spare their fellows [γένους],

17   ibid., p. 34.
18   ibid., p. 40.
19   ibid., p. 26–27.

for fear of falling under barbarian domination?"[20] For Plato, it is not even proper to refer to armed conflict between Greeks as "war"; rather, he prefers to call it "civil strife" to "reflect a real difference between two types of dispute. And the two types I mean are the one internal and domestic, the other external and foreign; and we call a domestic dispute 'civil strife' and an external one 'war.'" Thus, "when Greek fights barbarian or barbarian Greek we shall say that they are at war and are natural enemies, and that their quarrel is properly called a 'war'; but when Greek fights Greek we shall say that they are naturally friends, but that Greece is sick and torn by faction, and that the quarrel should be called 'civil strife'."[21] Such a relationship between Greeks of different *poleis* is natural because they share a religion and culture:

> "And won't they be friendly to all Greeks? And won't they regard Greece as part of their common heritage and share in the same religious rituals as the rest?"
>
> "Yes, most assuredly."
>
> "So that means that they will regard their dispute with the Greeks who share their culture, as a civil conflict and not even refer to it as a war, doesn't it?"
>
> "No, they won't."[22]

The unity of the *genos* is found in a common religious rite, a common heritage and common language. As Smith observes,

---

20   Plato, *The Republic*, trans. by Desmond Lee, (New York: Penguin Books, 1974) p. 257.
21   ibid., p. 258.
22   Plato, *Republic*, ed. and trans. by Chris Emlyn-Jones and William Preddy, vol. 1, (Harvard University Press, 2013) p. 531.

18

"For the greater part of human history the twin circles of religious and ethnic identity have been very close, if not identical. Each people in antiquity possessed its own gods, sacred texts, rituals, priesthoods and temples, even where minority or peasant groups might also share in the dominant religious culture of their rulers."[23]

Smith describes the notion of nation which has come to predominate in the post-Enlightenment West as a "'civic' model" which is "a predominantly spatial or territorial conception."[24] However, the traditional model of "an 'ethnic' conception of the nation" has as its "distinguishing feature" its "emphasis on a community of birth and native culture. … Whether you stayed in your community or emigrated to another, you remained ineluctable, organically, a member of the community of your birth and were forever stamped by it. A nation, in other words, was first and foremost a community of common descent."[25]

However, this so-called "traditional model" was already losing its sway in the West by the time of the rise of the Stoics: culture was developing a certain permeable character, at least as pertained to the *genos* of one's birth, and allowed 'outsiders' to become part of the community, despite having been born as members of a different *ethnos*, because a notion of a fundamental unity of humanity was gaining prominence. Hesiod had already identified all men now living as part of his fifth, or iron, race, and although the biological predestinarian views of Plato and Aristotle prevailed with a sense of vocational and ethnic distinctions being quintessentially natural in origin, the Stoics

---

23   Smith, p. 7.
24   ibid., p. 9.
25   ibid., p. 11.

reframed the discussion in terms of the fundamental unity of the human race. As Richter observes in *Cosmopolis*:

> ...the idea of the unity of humankind evolved in the fifth and fourth centuries as a response to and an engine for the creation of a rapidly shrinking and increasingly integrated *oikoumenê*. The horizons of the ancient world broadened during this period as the result of demographic shifts and the redrawing of ethnic, cultural, linguistic and political boundaries. In the fifth and fourth centuries BCE, the increased presence of outsiders in the classical city-state as well as the creation of sources of authority that lay outside of the *polis* destabilized the idea of the *polis* as a kin group (*natio*).[26]

The Stoic reconceptualized the understanding of the nature of the human soul, so that "the Stoics saw no different 'types' of human soul. This conviction grew out of a unifying physics that saw the universe as essentially one; Stoic physics, in turn, had ethical consequences that led ultimately to cosmopolitan political ideas."[27] Where Aristotle saw many different types of souls, "the Stoics rejected the idea that there are different 'types' of human souls and with it the hierarchical social and political structures that Aristotle advocated in the Politics and elsewhere."[28] This did not mean that the Stoics were a bunch of modernist universalists; rather, the Stoics reconciled their no-

26   Daniel S. Richter, *Cosmopolis—Imagining Community in Late Classical Athens and the Early Roman Empire*, (Oxford and New York: Oxford University Press, 2011) p. 6.
27   ibid., p. 66.
28   ibid., p. 67.

20

tion of the soul with an understanding that the realm of ethical
responsibility began within the sphere of one's *oikeios*[29]:

> Although the Stoics were not the first to use the verbal
> noun *oikeiôsis* and its cognates (the adjective *oikeios*, the
> active form of the verb *oikeioun*, and the middle *ouke-
> iousthai*), the Stoics did radically redefine its meaning.
> At the center of each of these forms is the Greek word
> for "house" (*oikos*); those people who are *oikeios* origi-
> nally referred to persons who were members of one's
> household, including those related by blood, marriage,
> and a host of other domestic relationships.[30]

This notion of *oikeios* then influenced other schools of thought.
Thus Arius Didymus (teacher of Emperor Augustus in the
first century B.C.) characterized Aristotelean Peripatetic ethics in such Stoic terms, expressing ethnic identification and
loyalty in terms of *oikeios*:

> In particular, Arius tells us that although we feel a
> natural affinity toward our own children, parents,
> brothers, wives, members of our household and fel-
> low citizens, this affinity is not the same in each case.
> We feel a natural friendliness (φιλία) toward those of
> our own *ethnos* and our own tribe (πρὸς ὁμοεθνεῖς
> καὶ ὁμοφύλους) and, indeed, toward all human be-
> ings (πρὸς πάντας ἀνθρώπους), but—and this is
> crucially important—our "common love of humanity"
> (κοινή φιλανθρωπία) is much stronger for those who
> are closest to us. ... according to Arius, the Peripatetics

29 "*Oikeiôsis* stands at the beginning of all Stoic ethics." ibid., p. 74.
30 ibid., p. 74.

claim that "we have, from nature (ἐκ φύσεως), different kinds of affinity for them."[31]

The Stoic understanding of the universality of humanity and the obligations of *oikeios* found expression in the writings of many philosophers over the course of centuries, but rarely was it given as eloquently as may be found in Cicero's *On Duties*:

> Then, too, there are a great many degrees of closeness or remoteness in human society. To proceed beyond the universal bond of our common humanity, there is the closer one of belonging to the same people, tribe, and tongue, by which men are very closely bound together; it is a still close relation to be citizens of the same city-state; for fellow-citizens have much in common—forum, temples, colonnades, streets, statutes, laws, courts, rights of suffrage, to say nothing of social and friendly circles and diverse business relations with many.

> But a still closer social union exists between kindred. Starting with that infinite bond of union of the human race in general, the conception is now confined to a small and narrow circle. For since the reproductive instinct is by Nature's gift the common possession of all living creatures, the first bond of union is that between husband and wife; the next, that between parents and children; then we find one home, with everything in common. And this is the foundation of civil government, the nursery, as it were, of the state.

---

31   p. 76.

Then follow the bonds between brothers and sisters, and next those of first and then of second cousins; and when they can no longer be sheltered under one roof, they go out into other homes, as into colonies. Then follow between these, in turn, marriages and connections by marriage, and from these again a new stock of relations; from from the propagation and after-growth states have their beginnings. The bonds of common blood hold men fast through good-will and affection; for it means much to share in common the same family traditions, the same form of domestic worship, and the same ancestral tombs.[32]

The Stoic view of *oikeios* provided a philosophical framework for conceiving of humanity as a "universal bond" in which the particularity of identity was formed in the context of a given culture. And one's membership in a particular culture was the fruit of *paideia*, the overall education which shaped not only one's knowledge of language, history, and the entirety of culture. By the time of Lucian of Samosata (A.D. 125–180), it was possible for a Syrian to deny that he was a barbarian precisely because—despite his *genos*—he had received the *paideia* of the Greeks.[33] The transmissible character of *padeia* was thus claimed to have freed it from its connection to a particular cultural center:

There is no need for the Syrian, in the period of the early Roman empire, to travel to Athens in

32   Cicero, *On Duties*, (Cambridge and London: Harvard University Press 1913) p. 57, 59.
33   Richter, p. 159.

search of this *paideia*; the viral contagiousness of culture makes the need for a cultural center obsolete. By placing his latter-day Syrian Anacharsis in Macedon rather than Athens, Lucian has subverted the Anacharsis narrative and the notion of cultural identity that it implies. *Paideia* is not the peculiar possession of the city of Athens; rather, its transmissibility allows a series of cultural centers.[34]

In *Early Christianity and Greek Paideia*[35], Werner Jaeger argues that the early Christian teachers utilized this notion of *paideia* in the formation of Christian catechesis. Thus, for example, for men such as Justin Martyr, the goal was to "speak to the educated few, including the rulers of the Roman Empire. They address them individually as men of higher culture (paideia), who will approach such a problem in a philosophical spirit."[36] In Jaeger's assessment, by the time of Clement of Alexandria and Origen, *paideia* and the Christian apologetic were thoroughly interpenetrated:

> The merging of the Christian religion with the Greek intellectual heritage made people reality that both traditions had much in common when they were viewed from the higher vantage point of the Greek idea of paideia or education, which offered a unique general denominator for both. We have found the idea of such a merger anticipated as early as Paul's speech in Athens in Acts, a book of broad historical vision, but it now

---

34   ibid., p. 171–172.
35   (Cambridge and London: Belknap Press, 1961).
36   p. 27.

comes to its full fruition. Origen's thought leads to a real philosophy of history, a thing that never grew on the soil of classical Greece because the Greeks of that period were concerned only with themselves and not with other civilizations.[37]

In short, in Jaeger's assessment, "Christianity ... now emerges as the heir to everything in the Greek tradition that seemed worthy of survival. It thereby not only fortifies itself and its position in the civilized world, but preserves and revives a cultural heritage that to a large extent ... had become an empty and artificial variation of a formalized classical pattern."[38] And as the *paideia* of the Greeks was once bound up with the conception of the *genos* of the Greek *polis*, now Christian catechesis is so linked with the emergence of the "new race" which is the Church. Thus, in the mid-second century, the question is posed in the *Epistle of Mathetes to Diognetus*[39]:

> I understand, sir, that you are really interested in learning about the religion of the Christians, and that you are making an accurate and careful investigation of the subject. You want to know, for instance, what God they believe in and how they worship him, while at the same time they disregard the world and look down on death, and how it is that they do not treat the divinities of the Greeks as gods at all, although on the other hand they do not follow the superstition of the Jews. You would also like to know the source of the loving affection that

37   Jaeger, p. 62–63.
38   Jaeger, p. 75.
39   http://www.ccel.org/ccel/richardson/fathers.x.i.ii.html

they have for each other. You wonder, too, why this new race [*genos*] or way of life has appeared on earth now and not earlier. … Now, then, clear out all the thoughts that take up your attention, and pack away all the old ways of looking at things that keep deceiving you. You must become like a new man from the beginning, since, as you yourself admit, you are going to listen to a really new message.

Commenting on this text, Buell notes: "… *genos* is redefined as that which is a marker of difference but potentially (if never actually) universal, like Roman citizenship. This slippage between ideas of ethnicity, race, and civic status would have been especially clear to ancient readers in relation to being Roman since Romanness is both a civic identity (linked to the city of Rome) and a broader ethnoracial one (in the context of the Roman Empire)."[40]

Membership in the Christian *genos* does not militate against a diversity of racial, ethnic, and cultural connections; thus we may read in the *Epistle of Mathetes to Diognetus*: "For Christians cannot be distinguished from the rest of the human race by country or language or customs. … Yet, although they live in Greek and barbarian cities alike, as each man's lot has been cast, and follow the customs of the country in clothing and food and other matters of daily living, at the same time

---

40   Denise Kimber Buell, *Why This New Race—Ethnic Reasoning in Early Christianity*, (New York: Columbia University Press, 2005) p. 31–32. However, it must be observed that there is much in Buell's overall argument which is highly reliant on current cultural obsessions regarding questions of race and ethnicity.

they give proof of the remarkable and admittedly extraordinary constitution of their own commonwealth." Christianity does not militate against such divisions; rather, it interpenetrates them. The faith does not militate against culture; rather, in each culture, the orthodox faith forms traditions which give expression to that which is believed. Such traditions may vary according to culture, but they should give expression to a common orthodox faith.

Icelandic philosopher Páll Skúlason begins his exploration of the 'conceptual network' for culture with a discussion of "the mind"[41] because he maintains that it is the irreducible core of self-definition: "Human beings are not bound to their culture, to a particular world or to a set of values or to a unique meaning of life. They are only bound to their own mind which allows them to travel through reality, to travel in all possible meanings of the term."[42] Here we find a universalism consistent with that which we have discussed in the context of Christian and Stoic thought. In this understanding, what is being asserted is that culture is not antecedent to mind, but this does not cause culture to collapse into post-modern relativism; that is, culture is not 'whatever we want it to be' or a naked assertion of the will in isolation. In Páll's words:

---

41   There is a deliberate ambiguity in Páll's use of the term 'mind,' which he maintains is equivalent to "the intellect, the soul, or whatever you like to call it". The point which is being established is the individual's capacity for self-reference in contradistinction to "nature" and "the other." Therefore, the ambiguity is introduced to avoid direct engagement in vastly larger topic of the source and essential nature of the mind/intellect/soul. See "The Idea of Culture" in Páll Skúlason, *Saga and Philosophy and Other Essays*, (Reykjavík: University of Iceland Press, 1999) p. 105–117.
42   Páll Skúlason, p. 106.

But I don't think it is wise to start with the mind and take it to be the centre of everything, a kind of sun around which culture, world, values and meaning are circulating. Of course, each human being is unique, but that doesn't make the human mind the centre of everything. There is something out there which is quite independent of the mind, I believe, the objective reality of what is called nature; and there is also someone or something out there who is not me but another me. This other me is also a mind, a spirit or a ghost, and she, he or it is an absolute stranger, not circulating around my mind, but rather reminding me that I am not the only conscious being in the universe.[43]

Thus, for Páll, to understand culture, "we can start with every-thing which is *different* from my mind. ... So in order to try to determine the idea of culture, we have to proceed from the idea of nature and from the idea of the stranger or the other."[44] Culture is thus born of an encounter with nature, and nature is never mastered. Since nature remains ultimately independent of our will, the "feeling of discovering nature as this totality" is "the only foundation of culture."[45] Thus, Páll declares, "the only real threat to the world of human culture nowadays is the fact that this feeling for nature is not properly respected."[46] Culture is thus related to a man's "three basic ways of relating to natural reality":

---

43   ibid., p. 107.
44   ibid.
45   ibid., p. 109.
46   ibid.

28

Theoria (contemplation), poiesis (production), and praxis (action) are all needed in order to secure human existence; they provide the material out of which culture is made and also the forms into which it is moulded. Most likely, men did not originally distinguish clearly between these forms of culture; religion, involving magic, worship and rules of behaviour, may require them all. Nevertheless, in Western cultures these three forms of cultural activity are clearly separated, and moreover, each of them is broken down into different parts which are often seen as opposed."[47]

Culture thus arises "because of people's estrangement from nature. Culture is a way of defining a domain of reality which provides people with a world of their own when they feel that their ties with natural reality have been broken. Instead of the natural world, to which we humans together with all other living beings belong, we now have the world of culture which is our world as human beings."[48] Because the distinction between *mind* and *nature* is inescapable, culture is a necessity of human existence, and a given culture is framed by a common sense of comprehension which stands in contradistinction to other cultures: the stranger who does not belong to our reality and thus does not share culture. Differences of *theoria*, *poiesis*, and *praxis* form the basis for different cultures. Thus, there are three "main conditions for a specific world of culture":

First of all we need space for *working* to take place. ... [T]he origin of the world "culture" is in agri-

47   ibid., p. 111.
48   ibid., p. 112.

culture. For this it is necessary to have a piece of earth, a country or, more simply, land. This reference to the land is of utmost importance. No culture has survived, to my knowledge, without some reference, ideal as it may be, to a specific land. ...

But the reference to the land is not enough and moreover, two different cultures may exist side by side on the same land, although not, perhaps, without serious problems.

The second element is *language*. This is necessary because of what I have called knowing, collecting and storing all kinds of information. Without language there is no way of keeping together the knowledge people need to have and to share for all their enterprises. ...

The last element required is *history* or ways of remembering in order to go on sharing the same ways of behaving. As the land provides organisation of space, history provides the organisation of time, of persistence and unity through time. As we all know, history is the basic means for transmitting culture. Every known culture has a collection of stories for narrating to children even before they can talk.

Land, language and history are the grounds for each and every culture. A living culture is a culture where people cherish *their* land, preserve *their* language and transmit *their* memories to new generations.[49]

This understanding of the three-fold ground of all culture leads to Páll's identification of the threat to culture in our own

---

49   ibid., p. 113–4.

age: "the incarnation of the culture that dominates our modern world, a culture under the spell of *Poiesis*, the culture of technology and of technological thinking. The great danger is that this overemphasis on *Poiesis*, of which the robot is the ultimate outcome, may in fact lead to the destruction of human cultures as they have developed so far. And then the secrets of the world, of value and the meaning of life—and of their underlying connections—may be lost forever."[50]

Thus there is not, nor can there be, a universal culture: even when there exists a broad commonality of cultural elements—common language, for example, or shared history—different cultures remain distinct. As Richard Weaver observed:

> ... any given culture is born, rises, and flourishes as an integer; that is to say, an entity striving to achieve and maintain homogeneity. It is this cohesive wholeness which enables us to identify it as different from other cultures, to give coherent descriptions of it, and to make predictions on the basis of these descriptions. Culture by its very nature tends to be centripetal, or to aspire toward some unity in its representational modes.[51]

The folly of imagining that a common *techne* will help to 'bridge' or 'unite' different cultures is readily evident: the invocation of "democracy" as a means for elevating the human condition across cultures is madness, and the attempt to impose a uni-

50   ibid., p. 116.
51   Richard M. Weaver, "The Importance of Cultural Freedom," in *The Paleoconservatives—New Voices of the Old Right*, (New Brunswick and London: Transaction Publishers, 1999) p. 80.

versalization of any culture in this fallen world must incline to disaster. Again, in Weaver's words: "Anyone who engages in cultural activity, however unconscious he may be of this truth, is testifying to a feeling that man is something more than a part of nature. And only when man has begun to create a culture does he feel that he has found a proper way of life."[52] The violence of a dislocation from one's own culture is an act of spiritual warfare which occurs when representatives of an outside culture seek to infiltrate and impose their culture on an existing resident population of a different culture.

In the context of each culture, there exist traditions which are necessarily linked to the preservation of the culture, and there is, within Christendom, a bond between tradition and the expression of the faith. In the words of T.S. Eliot:

> ... a tradition without intelligence is not worth having, to discover what is the best life for us not as a political abstraction, but as a particular people in a particular place; what in the past is worth preserving and what should be rejected; and what conditions, within our power to bring about, would foster the society that we desire. Stability is obviously necessary. You are hardly likely to develop tradition except where the bulk of the population is relatively so well off where it is that it has no incentive or pressure to move about. The population should be homogeneous; where two or more cultures exist in the same place they are likely either to be fiercely self-conscious or both to become adulterate. What is still more important is unity of religious back-

---

52   ibid., p. 79–80.

ground … There must be a proper balance between urban and rural, industrial and agricultural development. And the spirit of excessive tolerance is to be deprecated. We must also remember that—in spite of every means of transport that can be devised—the local community must always be the most permanent, and that the concept of the nation is by no means fixed and invariable.[53]

Eliot comprehended a point which the ancient Greeks did not: "Tradition by itself is not enough; it must be perpetually criticised and brought up to date under the supervision of what I call orthodoxy; for the lack of this supervision is now the sentimental tenuity that we find it. Most 'defenders of tradition' are mere conservatives, unable to distinguish between the permanent and the temporary, the essential and the accidental."[54] Perhaps it would be a step too far to say that tradition is always in flux, but tradition is certainly something which must adapt organically, for it is only then that it can serve orthodoxy. Again, in Eliot's words:

I hold … that a tradition is rather a way of feeling and acting which characterises a group throughout generations; and that it must largely be, or that many of the elements in it must be, unconscious; whereas the maintenance of orthodoxy is a matter which calls for the exercise of all our conscious intelligence. The two will therefore considerably complement each other.[55]

53   T. S. Eliot, *After Strange Gods—A Primer of Modern Heresy*, (London: Faber and Faber Limited, 1933) p. 19–20.
54   ibid., p. 62.
55   ibid., p. 29.

Eliot anticipated that the individualism which was already ascendant in his own age was the bitter foe of tradition and orthodoxy for he perceived individualism's idolization of the individual:

> What I have been leading up to is the following assertion: that when morals cease to be a matter of tradition and orthodoxy—that is, of the habits of the community formulated, corrected, and elevated by the continuous thought and direction of the Church—and when each man is to elaborate his own, then *personality* becomes a thing of alarming importance.[56]

When one's identity is not shaped by *cultus* and culture, then personality—the cult of the individual—will arise. Disordered men are those have been taught to have contempt for the particularities of their distinctive characteristics as members of given cultures. But Pentecost did not bring an end to particularity; rather, it gave a context for its sanctified continuity. In the resurrection, the Christian race may have no further concern for such matters. But as long as this world endures, matters of *genos*, *ethnos*, and *polis* will remain of immediate concern because they give definition to men.

The destruction of culture and the decline of orthodoxy are related phenomena. Attempts by so-called 'Identitarians' to restore the cultures of classical antiquity by stripping away Christianity from European society[57] are breathtaking facile. Thus, Venner's claim, as a twentieth century Frenchman,

---

56   ibid., p. 54.
57   e.g., Dominique Venner, *The Shock of History—Religion, Memory, Identity* (London: Arktos, 2015).

that "My holy texts are the *Iliad* and the *Odyssey*, the founding poems of the European soul. These poems draw from the same sources as the old Celtic and Germanic legends of which they supremely express the implicit spirituality"[58] is the bloviating of a poseur. In Jaeger's scholarly assessment, "Plato in his *Republic* had rejected Homer and Hesiod not as poetic fiction but as paideia, which for him meant the expression of truth. Against him the Stoic school had maintained Homer and Hesiod as normative expressions of truth in order to retain the old poetry as the basis of Greek paideia."[59] Orthodoxy is unchanging; the traditions of a given culture must change, but do so gradually. Transient evils are resisted by means of the orthodox faith and the traditions of the fathers—a faith learned and confessed, and body of tradition rooted in the language, in the soil, in the history of a people.

S.D.G.

---

58   ibid., p. 15.
59   Jaeger, p. 48.

www.ingramcontent.com/pod-product-compliance
Lightning Source LLC
Chambersburg PA
CBHW060531280326
41933CB00014B/3135

*9 7 8 1 8 9 1 4 6 9 5 8 9 *